AF335681

lament
for
then
and
now

by

alan scott

PublishAmerica
Baltimore

Hardcover 9781627720298
Softcover 9781630044824
PUBLISHED BY PUBLISHAMERICA, LLLP
www.publishamerica.com
Baltimore

Printed in the United States of America

for family, friends, and lovers...then and now

Other Books by Alan Scott

The Will of Our Times

Three Trends on Cue

Forever with the Veiled Lids

Dust and Clay

Just One of Those Stories

Though Youth is Gone

Rest Area

Silence

Vultures and Pigeons

Contents

the right to review

in this, the scheduled time of triumph

does anyone take peace so lightly

that the pistol-packing general with the varnished helmet

        circling the inquisitive mind

        who told the school children

that they were the legions of another war

spoke national peace?

listen!

listen to that next war,

the one some solar historian will call world war III

      (the one with the creation of planetary silence)

the last war

because beyond remain no more human ingredients for war

no atom bomb or radar-brained explosive

in the perpetually out-dated mechanics of war

is worth its making   unless

        there are humans to kill

        and cities to squander

        and cultures to dissolve.

once upon a time

only one space separated conflict from conflict:

        the time of burial

        the time of laying this war's dead over the last

the time of pruning for new ambitions

the time of replenishing material

the time of isolated hope

though assurance is only

that the next fire is again ours.

all this was

(if the expression has not grown a beard)

pre-hiroshima

pre-iraq

pre-atomic energy for military purposes

pre-world war II

pre-afghanistan

only some distant solar historian

can tell of the last war because here

no one can be left to record.

in hiroshima, afghanistan, iraq

(the dumb, ignorant, barbaric places)

the scribblers could find no one to describe,

since maggots, even in million-moted herds

revel in their own inarticulateness.

mass death in nothing new to the human race

since people have become addicted to dying that way

since they were shed by trees

and backbones brought them upright;

but no human gets used to it,

the permanence is too complete,

heart failure walks in laughing.

the barbarian losers being set ablaze from a safe distance

had a flaming succession of seconds

to wonder

        who did it

and why

        they did it.

should we tell them?

should we tell about

        the napoleons and hitlers and francos and stalins

        and huey longs and huesins who used physical

weakness

and moral indifference

to paint themselves backboards of selfishness?

or would divorce be better,

divorce from human commodities

        in our excuse to these people

and   speak   instead

of squalor   ignorance   desperation

that have jointly countered the futile hope

of the human barbarian

since christ walked on water?

when water walked alone

perhaps the barbarian losers

wants a shampoo of soap opera

where tragedy runs on endlessly and harmlessly

but is it too much like their lives

without the funds of all the NBC characters.

listen!!

listen to the next world war

the one the librarians will call world war III!

listen to the cruel stoppage of planetary heartbeat,

listen to the churning in graves of the others

who beat eternity to the punch

before man came

came and resolved himself

into a weapon capable of mechanic suicide.

the barbarian losers

who sat dazed in the bleak destruction of his bed

for that particular succession of flaming seconds

may have wondered what brought him to this,

should we tell him?

tell him about the nagasakis, the tarawas, the lexingtons,

the bull runs, the big bends the long marches across nations

like china

that brought him steadily to this?

or should we subtly and behind his back

bring in the adding machines for testimony

and total up the measureless sections of violence
that ended up in others like him?
should we do in 16 millimeter
the bleak road of bones on which the crusades staggered
or reasons for great walls of china?
or should we count out in fingers
the premature optimism
since 5000,000 b.c.
that sustained human hope?
shall we count the milk bottles
or the childbirths
or the veterans
or the abortions
or the birth and/or birth certificates
or the copulations in hidden places
or the immeasured anguishes of people too little or too desolate
to defend themselves.

if we run out of fingers
and the patience of species
we could add in red to the totals
the violence missed:

        like the people impaled on the spartan phalanx
        and the human bridges for early sultans
        and the cubic centimeters of protoplasm
        that built up the pyramids.

the dazed barbarian losers know them, all of them,

brethren whose ends tabulate as completely

and useless as his;

after them, count in this reproachful tabulation

the men who oar-chained magnificence of the roman navy

and the black men sold into slavery by other black men

and devoured in the odorous holds

of hired out ships

by disease that crept up their bodies like fire

and gave no peace…but one.

no matter that the divine

taught him to worship the dead

the relentless mill of human history

grinds these barbarians losers down into brotherhood

with the community of dead

the hiroshimite   the afghani   the Iraqi

should have had reprieve from his brothers

in exchange for backtearing hours, hours

turning over plants   dissecting weeds

stamping out numerical wealth for those

who think the machines are theirs.

if, instead of this,

he should ask his own questions,

they would wonder why

the force that goes into personal campaigns of glory
is not expended in something to do with him;
he might even know why the thomas paines,
and the spear-holders in the metropolitan opera chorus lines
usually get nameless graves
while those with the necessary selfishness
get monuments in the town square?

the occasional exception
like christ
            like lincoln
            like some billion other characters
who held off history by dying in it,
in scant consolation to this barbarian loser
sitting in his blaze of eternity and wickedness
by virtue of the war department of the united states
        (with the active participation of god)
and the combination of channeled human intelligence
and the enumerated brilliance of atomic power.

science continues its blind art of denying human inspiration
toward unscientific things like
equality of opportunity
and the right to live without special
pointing-out of the monster of atomic destruction
can only, mirrorlike, see itself;

the fifty million who lost their bloods' cursing

in international orgasms during our recent times

might be able to talk to these we oppose

in his final moment

and say:

        keep the faith

        the home fires, they gotta burn

        observe the golden rule

        the divine inspiration of god

        and god is kind...

history speaking

        (pause for station identification)

        do you think bub, that this is the first time you

        lost a war to yourselves?

reflect, son, and think of how many lost wars i saw,

        keep the trust

        little acorns into gigantic acorns grow

        if they get the time

but history's old stuff;

        and if they couldn't speak

        they would probably point out

        obscurities about other barbarian losers

        (which means any representative of this

         vast disaster we all call a higher order of species)

        or about the laden dowagers who hold up fatted hands

        against time

       and use fat and chocolate-laden bodies

       for re-inforcement.

or about the dutch boy and the dike

or the marine sitting on guadal grenades

to save two guadal guys who had seen none,

or: (just to vary the program)

the little slant-eyed guy in the mail suit

who fell against the samati sword in century

fifteen because someone told him to

and because even if he wanted to do something else

there were still the eleven slant-eyed little guys

and

       the lone slant of wife

      and   what passed for home.

the point: take all these bold streams

       and twist them into a single red current

then translate into hiroshima   afghanistan   iraq

and wonder

as

    i

      do

why we haven't passed our adolescence

in this, the scheduled hour of triumph

where is the triumph?

    where is the schedule?

    where is the hour?

that should have struck with shattering force

every passionate second of the costly time table

of human progress.

THINK YOU THAT ETERNITY WAITS FOREVER, SLAVERING?

lyric

life is
living slowly
death is quick in all
but
knowing it
has come.

heaven visits
with us.
it is always
here
but we discover
slowly
world
speed not away
hear me slowly
world:
SPEED NOT AWAY!

i've never seen war

i've never seen war, oh god forbid!

i've never seen war, a lost bastard kid

i've never seen men die,

their bodes rotting dry,

and the rains come

and fill their open mouths and a broken eye;

i've never seen that!

nor have i been able to cry when i've heard them say

how it is when buddies die,

the jims and johnies they knew so well.

they laughed and drank with

and together cursed hell.

that was the day before.

now they only remember the strewn, torn,

dismembered, burnt, brown bodies, and

i've never been able to cry.

       i've never seen war oh, god forbid!

       i've never seen war, a lost bastard kid!

I saw them go off to war,

i was (and am) just a kid

and they too were as young as I am now,

i saw them hold mothers near

and each of us dropped a tear

but it was like sending them off

to college or camp;

the letters were different and changed

more and more-then there were no more,

they did not die outside but within there came a change

(like morning's scared shining and night's merry sin)

i did not feel all that, but i have a past,

and they have more, and where i

can look back and view a town, they

can look back and view a nation.

they looked the same but acted different

when they came back from the war

when they came back from the war

and the country evened the score.

                    i've never seen war, oh god forbid!

                    i've never seen war, a lost bastard kid!

a thread on the sand

worldly events require wordless moments,

i would as lief go hungry

as touch the surplus mass:

a lexicographer thrust into protests

for the quiet thoughts penetrating

as i sit on the beach

our beach

and seaward direct the past times

that alone i sang

and when together we chorused ideas,

threw pebbles at pebbles,

at the lone branch hinged in the water

as if shadowing everything around

...but us

because single thread on the sand

draws not the surrounding events,

we are no longer pathetic drifts of delusion-

the touch remains ours...

a war christmas

we sit impatient, puzzled, pained.

we wonder what is being gained

by mortal man, who, all year round

sew deep his seeds in bloody ground

then when the holy day draws near

and carols strike upon his ear

he joins in worship with the throng

sings the loudest in the song

his voice rings with the words again

"peace on earth, good will toward men!"

what is "peace" upon this earth

and toward which men must there be dearth

of good will lent, not freely passed

to men of every human caste?

this "peace" is not that of any lord

it is the peace of hidden sword

of tongues too glib, of justice lost

where yet the weaker is tossed,

his crime? the ancient bidding knock

upon the door of freedom's gate.

god's peace is love, this peace is hate!

then may this be our christmas cheer

the lord's true course is ours to steer.

remember well with hands untied

we'll soon walk free head high with pride.

this world is ours we must not fail

to make a worthwhile peace prevail

for every creed and revel then

in "peace on earth, good will toward men!"

ever learn the WHAT
and not the HOW the WHAT became

bill was

> i'll take you by your worldly man
>
> if what you know is what be thinks
>
> is of facts and figures.
>
> he knows all books and people and things,
>
> could tell from all
>
> universities and libraries and things...

bill was

> they wrote-on-a-piece-of-paper
>
> an EDUCATED MAN
>
> who could insert all reasoning
>
> and still went out into life
>
> to apply his learning...

bill was

> approached
>
> one day by josephs
>
> who told bill that they
>
> knew that:
>
> > bill was a member of the intelligencia
> >
> > (yes, statistics knew bill of that)

       bill should protect the low commoners

       (protect, he found in the dictionary:

       shield from danger was good bill knew)

   josephs said:

       you should join us

       protect them here

       shield them here

       impoverished the condition

       here and there...

bill saw

     his facts and josephs' facts

     and joined the COMMittee

     because all he saw or ever knew

     or was taught was

     the GOOD and the PLEASANT

     when all people told bill

     that he was doing WRONG

     he would say:

       look at this and this and that

     and the people turned away to say:

ever learn the WHAT not the HOW the WHAT became

he knows the WHAT

but NOT the HOW

that made the WHAT

what the WHAT is

and never was taught how

to go from

WHAT TO HOW...

it was easy for bill

to fall-in-with

the COMMittee for:

bill was

only taught WHAT

in universities

and libraries

and things

BUT NEVER HOW...

purpose

Permeating bits of crumbled illusions

flighting through dead space forward:

experience

from basic elements

lasting shortly within

foreign commodities

and fading quietly

into vacuumed ages.

the rocks are adolescent

feeble

are

deposits for streams

streams for lakes

lakes for oceans

oceans for eternities

eternities for illusions

for

tempting shapes of space

relaxing on

      time past

      time present

      time future

and the beginning
is an end
within itself
replenishing itself
and nothing.

autumn is but a thought

to describe the possibilities of a season
    is to deal with nature as a habit
        thinking of only conscious places illustrated
        in the determined evidence:
thus a scaled platform of vague discontent
    stereotypes the hidden meaning: autumn
        becomes a mood.
apparent inconsistencies organize themselves
    into pressing tension
        considerable the more lucid affection
        of a change of seasons to seclusive crying.

autumn is but a thought
    regarding dominant appearances as punishment
        which escapes from our enactment of isolation.

there is the city

a few industrial ragged dimensions,
       blueprints assisting moral condemnation
              and amphyon's lute comforts the living

a bricked morphological peculiarity
       immune to a careful understanding
              inside is an associated system of mouths:

wires deducting well-covered faults
       while thru to a surface
              emerges an international fever
that marks the poison
       from what is known as
              home.

pre-commercial

sing thee,

oh nightingale

of the heart

and perform within

thy depleted range

the area of forgotten time

when hence

you discovered peering

through thy soul

the common towers

of love

and sacrifice....

dilemma

why is this
i cannot
think or act
i am not here
nor there.

they tell me what
i should
but i stand idle
and cannot understand:
this is the end
except
for
        LOVE.

no-parking blues for a poet

freely a balance was effected
>within resemblance of artistic value—
>>unexpected scenes fidgeted perhaps
>>in ceasing perceptible disorder dashed against
>>>the overlapping differential character
>>>>who you memorized in troubled
times.

A distracted mind and mimetic elements dance about
>but unto a glowing incantation there remains the disguise;
>>you were not a builder of images
>>but an image (pale and enslaved in unseated
>>>criticism)
>>outside the scope
>>>contemporary appropriateness
examined
>>>commercial value.

then you worked:
>altering the infallible test
>against all offensive tactics heavily attacked
struggle possessed
>importance discovered their formula restored

            unexplained states reduced control
and you
  the poet remain the jungle analogy
          carried further on a stage of upsets
              multiplied in not too substantiated an imagination.

an alien land

my paradise which dies nearby in the dim future
        thirsts in a legitimate independence wandering
                from purposeful actuality to informative exhibition;
my America
        is a cranky formula
                permitting the sudden magical thing to have a place
                where the savage offspring wage their wars
                        against obtrusive control
while contrary to the sky
        this idle decoration
                tolerates on the diversity of undoubted gain.

yes
        this association of many qualities
                wax-like itself interests in all products
                except the unalloyed products.

this country so far from itself is a rented extravagance
        signifying a monotony and legality
                that schemes with substantial caution;
an excessive family of parents stabilize values
        that for their children are limited noises belched
counterparts in allies tongues are to be silent:
        man-worship blocks out learning

remainders based chiefly from heathen expositors

of a diseased tongue searching the survival

of an idea…

prejudice

a seed

small indeed

was dropped to feed

in the dark cool earth

(note not its birth)

its root grew deep

as down they creep

unfurling its power

in the earth's own bower,

one good wrench

of hand in clench

could when young

(and limbs unhung)

stop its force

in its course.

and this spread and spread

but would be but dead,

none saw its influence

or could judge the consequence,

one has but to look and see

this weed has poison as its key

(but it grew large and wide

to be a tree hard to hide)

its dripping leaves not block the sun

few escaped the shade and fall being one

of many who must mend their way

cursed by the tree every day.

god's book

stale parchment

evolving in

un-heard of scriptures

finding solace revived in parables

in depleted ranges:

grotesquely absorbent in ages

that have no second

aged hand burning left

and to left finds no right

striving for shrilled

shouting something strong.

temporary caprice

captured for ageless seconds

from sparing moments;

in sight we see

in nature we take refuge

in heart we comprehend

in this we attribute.

a young sorrow

young men have a strange way

in which to say

their sorrow,

spending little time on

fearing tomorrow;

deciding in predicated wisdom sage

to squander no time on age

saying:

        that's ahead!

and:

        no jokes about it now!

the youth tackling the bmt at noon

hears elemental voices that soon

ripple out

in subtle doubt

with the selfsame urges

in the articulated surges

of brethren in battle

whose sad faces tattle

that

yesterday and tomorrow

are

inseparable;

that young men have a strange way

in which to say their sorrow
if
i could have any wish in heaven
i wouldn't care about always rolling seven,
just
give me for free
a conductor's jubilee
and
let him reign
over their special train…
i'd
wake them ten minutes
in every eleven

puzzle

the world slants down

at its own precaution

to sink and thread no more.

the sky looks upon the world

and can only sigh (and maybe wonder)

that the plant

             the animal

             the man

look up

and up and up

and

up

locating their own crushed and

devalued statures.

sonnet

those minds that reason not

but all are feeling

respond to the harps of wind

to every blow of fancy,

voicing in their moods

the flow and ebb of the ideal

harkening the sound of beauty

strained for distant lightening

of fancy diamond wings

they watch to follow

      wearying their feet in traveling as they go

oft-disillusioned they wait

for that delivering day when they shall

      be let forth in ravishment come real

for the blind striving of those oft-scarred

human hearts pursuing beauty ever onward

there is no place nor surfeit nor content

except perhaps in dreams

too long alone

and we dream of happiness that's always flown.

human folklore

the leaves have turned crippled crimson

but the parasitical mass remain lascivious

crumpling the myth

and making a litany of doubt

requiring justice and resolute impassiveness

as being the coverlet for our uncommunicableness.

the leaves cover the ground

wither...die...waste and are lost.

the psychopathic gods walk the streets

forever sympathetic with their own monstrous fragility

caustic incoherence

and invalidated philosophies.

the leaves are no longer a living symbol

but are gone.

a tear from eros's eye steadily descends his cheek

until it has reached

the cool

      hard

      earth.

lines

the seed

lusts for form of flower

with whom sun and rain

mind and heart

conspire to beget whirled perfection

on the empty air...

it is sorrow

not to share the triumphs of the rose

but be only as the grey rain:

shapeless

frustrate

arrowing at wind's behest

...the grey rocks

... the silent fields.

a discovery

(for the memory of Oscar Wilde)

i knew not for his flesh;

      a tipsy lad asking for manhood

            deranged in amourous speculations

as shelves of mouldy newspapers

      discovering thundered space

            cheating all fraudulent grace.

not one touch on his breast

      stealed myself against a broken word;

facial expressions from culture to culture

      was a graphic record

            of electrical charges anticipating his words.

former elements involved in pattern,

      this breath was no mechanism

            inducing startled affect in a general silent region

of geometrical figures puzzled

      with any analyzation of magnifications in their claim.

his kiss would not have been an experiment

      indicating strangeness of a blush

but rather:

      <u>a dilation of all habitation</u>

      <u>simultaneously pressing on an infant's cheek</u>

      <u>burning in a show of successions of waved phenomenon</u>

      <u>banded where the polished tributary of the surface</u>

<u>meet with the override of a margin.</u>

A statement is quite variable

losing balance observed among shadows

but closer to the world was his leaning development

dominant as a procession

which sets an hour given to conventional sun.

there are several reasons for this strangest of cards resisting

all forces of ambition with which i cultivate

but verdicts have enlightened peace;

condition akin to admiration navigate separately

framing   people   patiently

from themselves

as a discovery of Oscar

avow in the handiwork that consent

to bonds of a trackless miracle.

runaways

time flows, seasons drift for another year together,

orphaned emotions, our source of tears and laughing,

wander beyond that conscious age,

when scarcely our fleeting passion shaped a power

that bound to us the shape of brightness,

gathered as a cloud

rolled away the earnest face of despair,

blending love and fate and silent sea,

enchanting waves of purpose with the boundless

vibrating of what you needed

and i needed,

a communion with pure and strong spirit

as tenderness as a memory's theme,

rolling a daily tune and blending

the happiness which we and nature give.

My companion, my needed joy, my source of passion,

wander with me for another year

and yet another,

shift not our course to which we travel,

our mortal frames set toward a new land

with love's foundation as its start...

away at war at christmas

the night is dark

the tropic air is humid warm

and everywhere the stars in no stark make-believe

set the scene for christmas eve.

we're seated under god's own sky

the myriad of lights on high

illuminates to some degree

our lonely christmas revelry

it's hard to sing the joyous songs

when we've finished killing that morning

and when every heartsick man here longs

to see some white snow tonight

or to stand within the parlor light of home

to see his tree so warmly lit

with gay-wrapped gifts surrounding it.

it's difficult to sing tonight

our throats are choked

our nerves stretched tight

an empty cavern fills each chest

with christmas here

our tropic quest

vocalize

a pictured embrace whose still breath lingers'

past clouds timely engulfed in strings of a piano,

hammered with rust-tin age,

while a solo flute listlessly floats by uncontrolled space;

sky becomes blackened at times in the arms of god,

strike each other for one brief, eternal spastic second,

turn brown and red and black,

oh! so black with january thoughts,

blithed internal splendor that spreads throughout,

trembling loves throws nature to the fog,

and making both of us one line,

straight and transfixed,

prostrate feelings with dead grass spurting upward

mixing both for purity of sense,

while glass-cracked eyes peering into the fog

to the only revealing object: LOVE.

i, too, have grown upward spreading arms

to both left and right,

to both the horizontal and to a vertical,

my feelings on an upward plain-

to find, to touch to digest the revealing object,

i capture you and love.

recaptured blasphemies choked with lack

of sensual force or feelings sit with me

on a hill by the sea and roll subserviently down

into a gully of chambered thought;

in the death of leaves this moment pulses towards years

where a single moment cannot be defined

because added to it all makes our love the tiny peace.

perspective of afghanistan

what is this land,

a paradise or a stinking rock

or an oceanic pinhead

for senators to beat their breasts about?

could it be that it once was a paradise

when the olive-skinned folk lived their primitive life?

      the days before civilization made a mess of nature?

      the days before mankind made a mess of civilization?

      and the days before nothing was made a mess of.

it might have been a paradise

were it not for the stupid influence of egg-stuffed militarists

who think they stimulate the morale of the men

who seek to provide soft-cushioned chairs for the portly masters

of their corpulent cohorts

while the lesser (yet bigger) man sits on the ground to drink his beer.

it might have been a paradise were it not for the "efficiency"

this obtuse thick-headed efficiency

created under the mythical pretence of peacetime necessity!

necessity for whom? for what?

for the free american in war-worn khaki of his country

or for the convenience and comfort of the american von steubens

the military scientist whose greatest victory

was to feebly proclaim that trouser legs were not to be rolled up.

it might have been a paradise

were it not for the principles of caste

handed down from the legions of the aristocratic cult

which was disproved and dispersed at Lexington.

this caste divides american from american

not through allocation of responsibility or lucrative attainment

but through difference is social rank

which is socially rank.

it might have been a paradise

but it is a stinking rock!

but it is a stinking rock!

at my side

you came to me when I was on the
darkside of the moon,
furnished with crumbled illusions
designed from non-loving elements.

you saw a stoned container broken,
spirits deflated with needed repairs,
and patience was yours

you entered my life
as a ship enters rough waters,
without reservation for fear
of timbers breaking from the thrust,
undertaking the task of rebuilding
an identify that has gone aground.

for the evident restoration had to be extensive,
my will had to be acquired once again,
and so, my love, my birthday boy,
I want you to know that the repairs
have fully been made, I plead for patience
and continuance,

no longer do I look back,

but forward through any storms,

through any mishaps,

with you at my side.

passageway

hear thee

my auspicious burden

when thy frailty

and youth are

at a haste

to be finished

and forgotten

by those who did not

know

what they

desired.

we journey

not far amoungst

venus and sappho

but

rather

    to

        the

           depths

              below

where

my auspicious burden

thy frailty

and youth

will be finished...forgotten

thought 1

the charred and smoked indulgence

of so many a year

within printed pages full of dexterity

of heart and soul

that one looks for

only to be disappointed with complete

and unjust panic...

the guts for mankind are lost

being gone with thought

it is not better than one's picture frame

without a face or being

the lights coated with sentiment

go out

but darkness may also

be a form of the printed page.

thought 6

be lovely once again

when tears have dried to air...

remember to weep

before you have forgotten how...

this world knows too much of tears

yet knows not who cries or why it cries...

the world knows too little of laughter

and know not why it laughs...

Be lovely once again

the tears and laughter

    are here

    and everywhere

and one day they will disappear

    to

    air...

doomsday's reckoning

the hero awaits on the dry earth

to be let down to hell

where other conquers have gone

and remained still/quiet

pleasing death which conspires

with all the eternal audacities

that make the lonely rocks by the ocean

a liquid gelatin.

the ants and worms start their ceaseless occupation

the gnawing process of elimination

until the depraved nothingness of life is left

and the hero has become an abstract.

what next? And was it worth it?

the hero remains silent

his thick blood

which was once warm and rich

is forever a symbol of deterioration

and the vultures above become the outcast sylphs.

wavering

a single thread

for an eyeless needle

need not be compensated

for being the blunderer,

for within these translucent bodies

of solid complexities

man has lived

and the FAMILY has remained the whole

and the INDIVIDUAL has been lost.

time and a boy

it rains a luminous blood of subterfuge

waning indecision between

the leaf of mind and heart,

enclosing within its gargantuan strength

a peaceful repose,

for the rain is cold against his chest

with cruel arrows of pity for wetness,

and the tears on his cheek are the continuance

of this subterfuge,

in it lies a grieving boy

for the loss of his own unjust personality

which could one moonlight night

or graying dawn

find at last the lines on his face

of a shadow on the unobtrusive earth.

he will laugh again (after i kiss him)

this boy:

this symbol of so-chaotic-a-day;

vile gases will thin to perfume

industriously seeking a stronger clarity

ignoring the soaring feud and hates

(forgetting the foolishness of time)

and the rain will wash his tears

down the guttered paths of remembrance

reminiscing nostalgically

as if penetrating

far back into his mother's complacent womb

restoring or wanting for something indeed better

or at least

for that small speck of minute darkness

when we need something better.

A day remains a day,

the speck;

the boy is an entangled web

who supplements wine for water,

graves for havens construing to meet indecision

in the remotest ways,

while his blood continues to flow freely;

(bothering few when young, torturing many when old)

this subterfuge is continuously gnawing,

bringing about his out bursting droplets.

funeral

off a quiet promontory

on the swell

that's

wild and free

on the bosom of his ocean

with its soft

and lulling motion

like a gull

upon the waters

like the sea's immortal daughters

on a dark-beaked burning galley

midst the whisper of the sea

on the pillow of the deep

blazing to the gulf

of

       sleep.

homeward

look homeward thy orphans of a lost generation
to the inundations of this wild shattering splendor
that we know as being:

       the enfabled concrete of life we call the existence

       the planetary vacancy for crippled emotions

       the seashell of realities that has been washed ashore

       by the hissing glut of tides

       the exuberant optimism

       the brute fatigue

       the demented moralities that men have sweated for

       but have been tormented for-but remained

       their prerogatives as men

       the wasted excess which has stayed intemperate

       and within the unending fecundities

       the cockroaches have had a feast

       on man's ending growth and maturity

       within the farthest, the farthest and most remote adyt

       of his childhood

       the sinewy lines of all torrential discourse

       has continues disregarded until

       the unjust and huge imago descends upon us

       to make our passivity instant and permanent.

       look homeward thy orphans of a generation

lost in orgasmic conclusions wavering on indecision

never to realize their beauty or usability

and REMAIN IN THEIR IMPEACHABLE TUMULT.

hear ye! hear ye! john's forty

what does one say on this day?

do I breathe in the humorous

and exhale the remote?

can the world sell its limited expressions

and pass to you an impulse

to commit the next forty years

to vanity, or service, or folly, or moralizing

or a host of designs with disposable riddles?

when do you take us out of the center

in the circle,

and thrust to the outer edges

all the levels of love

which i have

even with your impenetrable reluctance?

what does one say on this day?

NOTHING... but bless you just the same.

in terrorem

first land stood then seas covered

land stood no more then land placed its shining face

upward ascending to leveled heights

while love (always fearless and speculative)

weakens abnormalities assailant of schism

profanes deviance thoughtlessness

classic notes with dimensions are placed by retired dangers

motion of time is a string pressuring oscillations

that are receptive to a property of simple consistent tones

new innovation of principles are laid over the untutored people

originally the strongest fortress...mistuned temperaments

arise to block the view

progress spits a secure dust from the storm

and who can tell when the repairs are attempted.

o tempora! o mores!

it should not follow that sound minds re-establish

themselves in a shaded hall of awardees

displays of wit should be found in pawnshops

natural abilities of the prepared me (as:sator resartus)

will return to the land instead of a panic of seas

which cover a voice of people.

echo

childhood whispers an echo to me,

greedily inventing a mirrored find,

casting on the beach the total freedom,

playground for running communities,

arranged for a challenging task-

jump and lie in the pacifism of an

inviolable citadel...

the disappointments come later

when the elusive image consume

our organization and murmur

the skeptical matters:

graceful and over-whelming sand castles

thin-down to a waiting echo,

attempting to renounce our instincts.

condensed novel about two boys

no matter the great barren land

    these two needy tissue-paper boys

        nourish a carried purpose,

adventurous in their devotion

    amplified

in sober statistical response

    they chase the sound of autumn

brought with a whispered cry

    or curdling minds engaged

        by kneeling intolerance of tight reason.

claude be one who is love

    snubbed by dreams,

        unnecessary at dawn

but divine in sunset

    pitching exaltation

        to squirming stars.

lance revolts at cradles

    and the dying

        escape of walls

losing a silent laugh at every turn.

    both leveled from abnormal grief

        unhealthy messengers departed.

change concerns the courageous
       healed by provocative efforts,
but claude with lance bereave
       the cobwebs of human revolt
           self-centeredness walks through
           their liturgical hymns.
pride and limitation and respect
       and development anger confidence
           that is painful fashion
           prematurely unwise in the wilderness
              of expression
planned shield of season
       burst and renew their tendencies-
           the people admirable with virtues reviewed
           denigrate in long-term employment
of specific amenities possibly reserved
       the huge gains are piled (and piled)
           like plaintiffs concluded.

knowledge is voted   hurdled
       some is purchased
           but times to venture these two:
       searchlights cast aside by weary tourists
           impressive in a wistful aloneness.

moods twist these pages of deranged value
        bemoaning the tang retained in all scenes.

our boys become naked in judgment far removed
        in their own vicissitudes,
                somewhere a brute wilderness makes legend on a
path:
the hideous skulls causing a quiet crisis
        bemuse far   away
    their effective faith-deluded   remote   abstract.

bleach thrown to dust saturates.

a plea for the people who run away

there are times my cohorts of encouragement
    when uncritical reflection produced by a slap
        from the mothers within us proceeds a series

of visions   and nutrition
    from a mere impulse scales a primary passion.

we in varying degrees conjecture vivid currents
    with suggested inferences(which become)
        the isolated lines of demarcation
        multiplied in commoner triumphs.

where meditation can never be possible
    suggestibility sinks first an automatic reverie
        of the inner persistent message   (written)
        as a direct creation in sequel form

haunted by impulses to appear
    excursions are made but visible theories migrate
        to all visual splendors that studied
        are rare as a habit is rare—
            indispensable as one's body unexplained.

We touch a value sufficiently skilled

      furnishing diverged successions   (but never)

         into a conception of the <u>jus naturae</u>

         growing as soil clothed in freshness.

All for each to his turn

      asylummed proofs are a written order

         provisions guard their lost-mentioned state.

it might be an end for resting people

      had otherwise repeatedly they run:

         theirs is a special favored circumstance

            stubborn and loyal to a contemporary.

rodeo with progress

saddle up the century!   spit blood from teeth
        of moments plagued (with plucked fired) diminishing
                as the shame of want.   converse with the day,
pray at the waist haste brother in free-denied spirits
        utmost rendered in his neighbors thrust
                heres labour partner-assigned precedence over
seasons
(her industry scaling the uncloud birth) chills rise above
        the clouds   precepts dispose in forfeited streams
                spurs tinkle as bribed children jointly screaming:
SHOW THEM THERE   THAT   WE IS STRONG   !!!

first whole hearts then cut plows
        losses make stitched shivers in cowboys minds:
                comfort is a silent grain grabbed at best from any
                rain   pointed to the sheltered hours
soaking horns that solicit scrutiny wanting expulsive stuff
        swimming together in silent-flown fall
                we are the makers of them all.
say bud
        its your turn next to jump the bull
                feel tired   feel alive   feel
anything!
gnash your teeth of aged weeds

> pushing back that harsh-grown flock of hair
>> buckle tight the shortening pain,
sweat   tear   cry
> break day on high.
here the fruitful area employed by doubt-hard sun
> rest in sweat converging on a prayer
>> imposing fleeced beasts deeper into season
>> prompted by a god.
look at heavens clear length,
> convectional bursts pop from an evening star
>> there is a slight cross made in a little spot
>> in the gouged dirt,
a cross that endures cowthings   horsethings
> peoplethings
>> a guest of forewarnings feasting on all friends.
american all   americans altogether
> like flippant monks wirebound in custard pies
>> exiled promptly into western civilization lies
torrent determination boxed in spectacle code
> enveloped in reputation.
>> echo's continue with tremendous inertia
frequently the permanent bridges of formalized movement
> boiled under by fingers of a river
>> detailed in cabinets of our own hells.

there is silence   there is dead silence

eyes are marshmallow in a genial warmth of horror
        that gaze on new-born as lion-dogs in their
        rigid mask
commissioned to store golden fields of a century
        led to awe by a cryptic sentence of an acolyte:
        ONE WILL GET HURT   ONE MIGHT EVEN DIE
        I HAVEN'T SEEN ONE DIE FOR OVER A YEAR
        YEP, THE COW JUST MIGHT MAUL HIM TO BITS
        THERES A BOY DYING ALL THE TIME   BUT
        WHEN I WAS A BOY IT WAS DIFFERENT (A WHOLE LOT
        DIFFERENT). IT WAS ROUGHER AND PEOPLE DIED BETTER!!!
these words astraddle a common people
        supine in the streets of all evil—
                faces that remain
                tenacious   troubled stoic.

time opposes the condition enterprising a pilgrimage
        of housed thoughts   however stated
                an adult population
(responsible as the quiet suppliant praying over the children)
        flashed in staged diplomacy.

the investment of this crowd is paid off:
        the brahma is hearty   the man too weak
                he sits as yak butter

pieced together from other bruises knifed in his heart

     from lack of inspiration;

<u>a job is a job!</u> is his eternal damnation

     <u>i have to make the most of it!</u>

     THERE IN THE HALF-LIGHT HIS PRAYERS ARE TO THE SKY...

all my boys roam

birth comes as a ridiculous speech to my boys
    when cold-bloodedly they begin implanting
      their delicate beauty as metaphysicians
or the street gamins comparing a state of consciousness
    with the memories slowly spin.
        a patch on an eye of local indifference separates
        my perceiving specks and prior to all amputations
        that will take place
they remain preached and employed by suspicion
    which is meted out by unhappy maidens of parenthood
    my boy poets and boy farmers have found
a terrible and total vengeance in the adult masters
    still-born in their legendary functions
      knowing too well that dicaepolis with homer
      were mere silent mummeries as the _mos maiorum_
splices a boy's origin of nature with the sphere of intent.

an exiled hymn is sounded
    it retains a council of moods chorusing
    a tragic undoing:
WE STAND AS PARENTS OF YOU ALL! (note well their gall)
AND KNOW THE BEST! (before the rest?)
IN PAIN   WITH BRAIN   (they speak and bruise the cheek)
WE KNOW THE BEST!!

WE KNOW the best!!!
WE know the best!

allowed to talk the listeners remain ratiocinative
      clamped in an utterance over-drawn
            my boys roam   at last!
            to cast the absolute vision distinct
from impossible fashions   fabliaux   that become
      exhaustive   and   remote.

poem for the one-night stands

thru insanity of open-mouthed oceans:
      awnings of a heart without words
         smoked admissions in a bursting forehead
is this love you bring!
bruises seep this mountain of muteness
      dislocated at every quiet touch
         recompensed to contended heights
and i
      i flatly dance in a prayer smudged
         by the blind dusted people.
hands that stagger in a parade of anxiety
      are placed on the begging slopes
         insinuations are in a valley
deep   so   deep
veiled cravings smile
      with you beside. it is
         forgotten soon.   it is
         forgotten too soon
            too soon...

forever with the veiled lids

sleeping children dramatized into adults
     accompany not an allegory of the dawn   .instead
       there is the building   up   that strikes
the ants in aegina as zeus ponders his display
     convincing not the fathers of actuality worshipped,
       time thins all defied dead men and opinions of these
loosen violence
("becoming out of nothing...") unharmed night wakens to the detail
falling origin of the death slain
     into a body of day.
       ancient whirring noises steadily decreased
mangled shapes pie shrouded in absurd ceremonies
     here loosed-tongue gargantuan flighting
       thru notes of sound seemingly thread-bare without
dread
       blending equally with the inner elements
come living fog   with lips
     of a first citizen (an average fellow) thinking
       undoomed thoughts   recommending customers
with chocked sentiment:
     here is a retailer of ingratitudes
       sipping stones quenched with human pride
(the actual cost comes by percentage)
     his empire polluted in the divine architecture

        of mechanism   diverted from a straight line
of consequence that is further approached
      (by fear) propagated in a perpetual lethargy.

this cries the citizen:
      THE REPUBLIC FOR WHICH I STAND
      IS MYSELF   AND ONLY MYSELF
      ALONE WITH MYSELF...
(who is)
      neither banker   neither educator   neither
priest
         but trafficked in cargoes of full hope
         dealing with all cloistered occupations
and vocations
       (as if) dervishes holding up for themselves a
         foreign conquests of seas east of their own shore.
hardered humanity moves with a delirium of insufferable desire
       that issue reflection from keen doctors recipes:
         --in chlorosim quam vulgus pallidos-colores
         aut febrim amatoriam appelat
(the laughter is soon retired)   somehow cures
       adorn this citizen at every improved turn
         midst a frontier of detached uncommunicableness
(climbing the flecks   which gape
       at the blessed with beverage
       on one pulse   disaster in the other

juggled back:

      a trembled mower

      over and over

      the singing grass.

courses which inherit this unbound pride

      where again he tries to hide

            people remain brave in this mourning hour

but somehow for our first citizen they are tiny lips

      of noon-blast frost running ploughed

            over himself.

civilization is punk   there are mysteries

of the drunk

      but those arte buried before a rite

            of daubing   (and afterwards)

echidna and geryon

            (the tiny monsters)

            bring forth a translation of our fates.

this citizen   this average fellow   remains

      forever with the veiled lids

            sandwiched in by fetish stone

            that lastly thrown

flame in a human sacrifice

      the sleeping children into adults

            cry in elemental cadences.

CPSIA information can be obtained at www.ICGtesting.com
Printed in the USA
LVOW051713090613

337615LV00002B/20/P